Minnesota

impressions

photography by Greg Ryan and Sally Beyer

FARCOUNTRY
PRESS

Right: White Bear Lake.

Title page: Pillager Lake.

Front cover: St. Louis River as it cuts through Jay Cooke State Park.

Back cover: Sioux quartzite boulders and prairie grasses, Blue Mounds State Park.

ISBN: 1-56037-288-5
Photographs © 2004 by Greg Ryan and Sally Beyer
© 2004 Farcountry Press

For more information on our books write: Farcountry Press, P.O. Box 5630, Helena, MT 59604; call (800) 821-3874; or visit www.farcountrypress.com

Created, produced, and designed in the United States.
Printed in China.

Left: Lily pads and reeds on Lake Namakan, Voyageurs National Park.

Below: A solitary brown-eyed susan in Hyland Lake Park Reserve, near Bloomington.

Above: Whitetail fawn relaxing in a field of wildflowers. PHOTO BY LISA & MIKE HUSAR/TEAM HUSAR.

Right: Sioux quartzite boulders, only part of the historic geological resources seen at Pipestone National Monument.

Left: Summer sun illuminates every detail of wood and masonry.

Below: Veterans memorial reaches skyward.

Above: Back roads through fall foliage, near Willow River.

Facing page: Pumpkins for sale—buy one or a trailer-full.

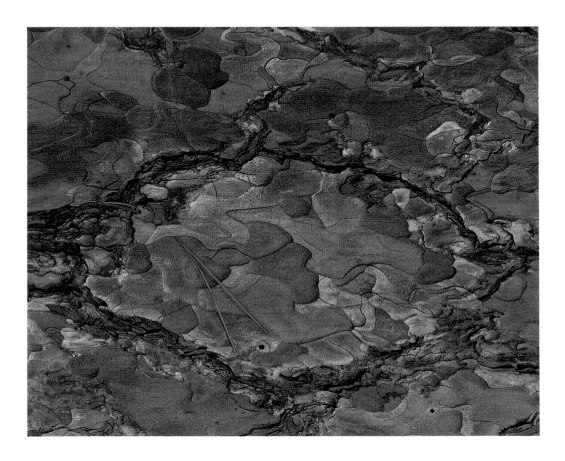

Above: A single piece of red pine bark exhibits a full palette of fall colors.

Left: Mille Lacs Lake: a powerful call to fishermen.

Facing page: A frigid Kettle River flows through white birch in Banning State Park.

Below: Split Rock Lighthouse guided Lake Superior ships from 1910 to 1939.

Left: Highlands of Superior National Forest: the fall view from Oberg Mountain.

Below: Straight and narrow traveling through central Minnesota.

17

Facing page: Spruce and bedrock look down on Lake Superior, Tettegouche State Park.

Below: Bathing boys, a detail of the Clemens Garden centerpiece, St. Cloud.

Right: The sun rises quickly to a still moment at Minnesota Point.

Below: In winter's clutches: Grand Marais Harbor.

Right: Relics of earlier farming days fade gracefully near Lake Vermilion.

Below: Kawishiwi River rapids beckon kayakers to the Boundary Waters Canoe Area, Superior National Forest.

Left: Afton State Park gives a forested perspective on the St. Croix River Valley.

Below: Lichen thrives on Lake Superior bedrock near Grand Marais.

Above: Mille Lacs, the second-largest lake in the Land of 10,000 Lakes, draws visitors year-round.

Right: August weather hovers above this reproduction of an eighteenth-century farmstead.

Left: Snow, ice, and water intermingle as the St. Croix River begins to thaw near Taylors Falls.

Below: Canada goose in late summer.

Above: Red fox curled up in the forest. PHOTO BY LISA & MIKE HUSAR/TEAM HUSAR.

Facing page: Great River Bluffs State Park rises above the Upper Mississippi River Valley.

Previous pages: Morning sun reflects off the St. Paul skyline and Harriet Island Park.

Right: Many visitors have fond memories of vacations at Burntside Resort, near Ely.

Below: One old Mille Lacs fishing boat is now the home of marigolds.

Above: A study in sharp angles: the historic courthouse at Stillwater.

Right: Duluth, Lake Superior's southern port city, grows up from the shores.

Above: Icicles on sandstone along the Kettle River, Banning State Park.

Left: Nineteenth-century railroad worker cottages survive intact in the Milwaukee Avenue Historic District of Minneapolis.

Above: Remains of Fort Ridgely, constructed in the 1850s on the Minnesota River, front the State Park's interpretive center.

Facing page: The Cascade River rushes on its way to Lake Superior.

Right: Reeds at sunrise, Lake Kabetogama
near Chief Wooden Frogs Campground,
Voyageurs National Park.

Below: A permanent mark of early Americans
at Jeffers Petroglyphs State Historic Site.

Above: The St. Croix National Scenic Riverway,
a favored canoe thoroughfare in summer.

Left: A silhouetted maple in an autumn dawn,
Mille Lacs Lake.

Above: The view from on high, at Blue Mounds State Park.

Right: Lake Kabetogama, rich in history—and fish.

Left: Contours in color: south-central farming country.

Below: There should be some greener grass on the other side.

Facing page: Gooseberry Falls State Park, known for its thundering river.

Below: Grand Portage takes us back to the fur-trade era.

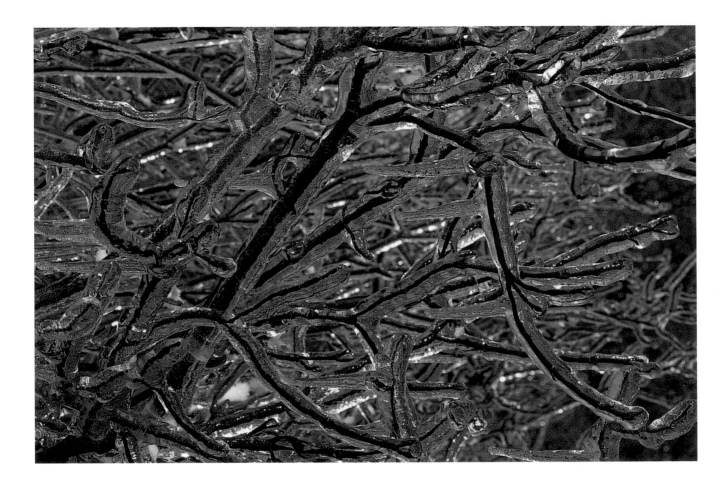

Above: This red dogwood may be encased in ice for the rest of the winter.

Facing page: The state capitol building, St. Paul, hosts Fourth of July fireworks.

Above: Gas station, bar, and restaurant on the way to Crane Lake lure you in.

Facing page: Regatta and the *Vista Queen* share a brisk day on Lake Superior.

Left: Working the Upper Mississippi, near Winona.

Below: Monarch butterfly and sunflower—color coordinated.

Facing page: Winnewissa Falls splashes lazily through Pipestone National Monument in summer.

Below: Lake of the Woods is 80 miles across from this spot in Zippel Bay State Park to the opposite shore in Canada.

Not to be lost in the winter white,
a farm near Magnolia.

Above: Good sledding from St. Mary's Catholic Church, New Trier.

Facing page: The Cannon River flows cold below the Welch Village millpond

Above: The American lotus flowers in July and August in the Upper Mississippi River Valley.

Left: Secluded Bear Head Lake State Park, where you might find black bears, nesting eagles, timber wolves, or moose.

Facing page: Itasca State Park, established in 1891, is considered the headwaters of the Mississippi River.

Below: Catch of the day: brown trout.

Facing page: The Pickwick Mill, constructed of local limestone in the mid-1850s on Big Trout Creek in southeast Minnesota.

Below: Bear cub wrestling with a tree.
PHOTO BY LISA & MIKE HUSAR/TEAM HUSAR.

Right: Rice Creek Chain of Lakes Regional Park, close to the Twin Cities but a world away.

Below: A day begins in absolute calm at Eagle Nest Lake Number 4, near Ely.

Above: Carnivorous pitcher plants await an insect meal in Lake Bemidji State Park.

Facing page: Ice-coated pebble beach along Lake Superior.

Following pages: Excursion boats float down the Mississippi to Minneapolis.

Above: Sparrow hawk chick in early spring.

Left: Shovel Point, on the icy edge of Tettegouche State Park.

Sally Beyer was born and raised in Wisconsin, but she fell in love with Minnesota soon after finishing her education. When Sally met Greg on a backpacking trip several years later, they discovered a shared interest in photography and eventually agreed to form a business partnership to make and sell beautiful images. Although Sally now spends much of her time tending to administrative and marketing tasks, she still manages to join Greg on a number of photo shoots and is especially passionate about garden photography. Sally lives with her husband in a log lake home near the eastern border of Minnesota.

Greg Ryan was born and raised in Minnesota and has always loved the outdoors. After earning a degree in forestry, he worked in land surveying for many years. An extended trek in Nepal taking photographs of the landscape and the people convinced Greg it was time to change careers, and he followed his heart and began a photography business with Sally Beyer. Their business offers assignment and stock photography, with an emphasis on landscape and travel. This will be Greg and Sally's fourth book. In 1994, they authored a photography book about Minneapolis and St. Paul, Minnesota, *The Twin Cities Naturally,* revised in 2001 as *Minneapolis and St. Paul.* The following year, Greg created a book of Minnesota landscapes, *Minnesota: The Spirit of the Land* with writer Doug Wood. In 2001, Farcountry Press published Greg and Sally's photography of Minnesota places entitled *Minnesota Simply Beautiful.*